Living off the Land

IN WEST IRELAND

TRANSLATED FROM GERMAN BY JANET ANN GOLDEN

teNeues

A WEEK AT SCREEBE HOUSE

Living off the Land

AND THE SEA. AND THE LAKES.

When I spent some time in Ireland during the 1980s, I noticed the great quality of the food of Connemara, the westernmost tip of Europe. It wasn't that the Irish ate nothing but healthful food—not by a long shot—but the quality of the food was excellent.

At that time Ireland was a poor country, and Connemara was one of its poorest regions. But anyone who knew their way around a fishing pole, grew a few vegetables in their own garden, and went hunting in the winter could nourish themselves healthfully on seasonal foods, even if money was tight.

The decade that followed was one of fantastic economic growth for Ireland, and consequently many people no longer ate food produced locally. Instead, they bought mass-produced food at the supermarket—and sacrificed quality in the process.

The "slow food" movement has seized on an idea that was already a given in the daily life of western Ireland's poor: preserving traditional methods of producing food, returning to regional products, farming livestock appropriately for each species, and maintaining a wide variety of flavors.

This book will take you along on a journey to an historic estate in western Ireland. Screebe House is known for its hospitality, convenience, and excellent cuisine. Hunting, fishing, and using natural resources have always played an important role here. This book tells you about them, too. We will show you how, with local products and a bit of talent in the kitchen, you can prepare wonderful meals reminiscent of Irish cuisine and the world of Ireland's rural population during the 1980s.

NIKOLAI P. BURKART
OWNER OF SCREEBE ESTATE

EVEN SEEN FROM AFAR, THE SCREEBE ESTATE GLOWS AGAINST THE BACKDROP OF ITS UNSPOILED NATURAL SETTING IN COUNTY GALWAY.

Contents

DAY 4

DAY 5

DAY 6

DAY 7

GOOD TO KNOW

A Week of Good Cooking at Screebe House

DAY 1

RECEPTION

the one and only

Screebe
the one and only

AN IRISH DELICACY

Fresh Oysters

WITH SCALLION-CHILI DRESSING

INGREDIENTS (SERVES 4)

12 fresh oysters
1 bunch of scallions
2 small chili peppers
3 tablespoons + 1 teaspoon / 50 ml white wine vinegar
2 tablespoons sugar
Salt
Pepper

PREPARATION

Wash the scallions and cut them into tiny rings. Halve the chili peppers, remove the seeds and dice them. Place the scallions and chili peppers in a small bowl and add the vinegar and sugar to taste.

Allow the dressing flavors to blend, then drizzle the dressing over oysters on the half-shell.

BRAZEN HUSSY II
GALWAY
JOHN 087 757 1320
PENN

IRELAND'S SPECIAL GEOGRAPHICAL LOCATION–AT THE MEETING POINT OF THE COOL NORTH ATLANTIC WATERS AND THE SOUTHERN SPHERE–MEAN THAT FISHING PLAYS A MAJOR ROLE IN ITS COASTAL AREAS.

SWEET AND NUTTY

Fresh Scallops

WITH OIL AND LEMON JUICE

INGREDIENTS (SERVES 4)

12 scallops, in their shell or shelled
Olive oil
Lemon juice
Pepper
Salt

PREPARATION

Open the scallop shells and scoop out the flesh, then clean them and cut them into pieces. Arrange the scallops in their shells. Sprinkle with oil and lemon juice and season with salt and pepper to taste. If you are preparing more scallops, it is a good idea to mix a dressing from the ingredients listed above.

Tip: Serve the scallops with salad and lemon wedges.

FRESH FROM THE SEA

Ireland's sweet and salt waters afford a wide choice of fish and seafood. Salmon, clams, lobster, and crab can be found on almost every menu and always play a key role in the local cuisine.

SHRIMP
Ireland has its very own shrimp festival. The Dublin Bay Prawn Festival, held every year in March, celebrates Dublin's coastal shrimp. But shrimp is also important to Connemara and figures in many recipes.
Peeled and precooked shrimp is available for sale, but it is also easy to prepare at home. To do this, first separate the head from the body with a twisting motion. Take off the remaining shell all the way down to the tail by separating it from the meat with both thumbs. The black vein on the back has to be removed. The best way to do this is to make a slight cut in the back with a sharp knife and pull it out.

SEA URCHIN
In Ireland, sea urchins are raised primarily for export. The gonads of the sea urchin are considered a delicacy particularly in the Mediterranean countries and in Asia. However, they are showing up on Irish tables more and more frequently. The roe is eaten raw, ideally with fresh bread and a few drops of lemon juice. To obtain the roe, cut a circle from the underside of the sea urchin and remove it. The orange gonads can be eaten right from the shell, but they also make a nice addition to salads or omelets. The taste varies and is often described as salty and similar to that of oysters.

LOBSTER
Irish lobster meat has an especially good structure, but remains tender with a certain sweet taste and exceptionally juicy, white flesh. You will need to simmer the lobster for 15 to 30 minutes to work with it. (Precooked lobsters are also available from fish markets, but they should be extremely fresh.) Allow the lobster to cool and then remove the claws from the body in a twisting motion. Break off the tail and carefully pick out the meat, removing the bowel. The claws can be cracked open with a heavy knife on a work surface; the meat can be removed there, too.

CONNEMARA'S LANDSCAPE ALTERNATES BETWEEN VAST MOORS AND HEATHLANDS, ROCKY COASTLINES, AND BODIES OF WATER LEFT VERY MUCH IN THEIR NATURAL STATE.

A QUICK BITE BETWEEN MEALS

Simple Ham Sandwich

WITH BLACKBERRY JAM

INGREDIENTS (SERVES 2)

4 slices of Limerick or cooked ham
2 slices of whole wheat bread
2 tablespoons butter
1.8 oz / 50 g arugula
3 tablespoons blackberry jam
Sprouts for decoration

PREPARATION

Limerick ham is traditionally smoked over juniper branches, immersed overnight in cold water, boiled in cider, and then baked to a crisp in the oven. This is the best recipe for anyone lucky enough to get a few slices of this ham, but it also works with conventional cooked ham. Take two slices of ham and roll them up. Butter the bread. Wash the arugula, select the best leaves, distribute them among the pieces of bread, and then place the rolls of ham on top. If you like, warm the blackberry jam quickly in a pot and garnish the sandwiches with it. Finally, top them with a few sprouts.

WARMING AND DELICIOUS

Apple Crumble

WITH ALMONDS

INGREDIENTS (SERVES 4)

¾ lb / 350 g apples
1⅔ cups / 200 g flour
2⅓ cups / 200 g ground almonds
⅔ cup / 120 g sugar
1 cup / 240 g butter, softened
4 tablespoons sliced almonds

PREPARATION

Wash, peel, and core the apples. Finely slice them and lay them in four small baking dishes. Mix the flour, ground almonds, and sugar in a bowl. Dot the mixture with the butter and knead it by hand to form crumble. Spread over the fruit and sprinkle with the sliced almonds. Bake in an oven preheated to 400° F/200° C for about 20 minutes until the crumble is golden brown.

COUNTY GALWAY'S CAPITAL ABOUNDS WITH STREET MUSICIANS WHO ARE MASTERS AT THEIR TRADITIONAL INSTRUMENTS.

HEALTH
EVERGR

A Week of Good Cooking at Screebe House

DAY 2

A FRESH AND LIGHT APPETIZER

Irish Mixed Greens

INGREDIENTS (SERVES 6)

5.3 oz / 150 g fresh spinach leaves
5.3 oz / 150 g seasonal field greens
1 handful of cherry or grape tomatoes
1 red onion
1 handful of mixed nuts
2 tablespoons olive oil
4 tablespoons white wine vinegar
Salt
Pepper

PREPARATION

Wash the greens and spin them dry. Wash the tomatoes and cut them in half. Cut the onion crosswise into rings and toss it well with the spinach, salad greens, and tomatoes.

Toast the nuts in an ungreased skillet.

Make the dressing from thee oil, white wine vinegar, salt, and pepper. Serve the finished greens with the nuts.

HEAVEN ON A PLATE

Clams

IN CREAMY WHITE WINE SAUCE

INGREDIENTS (SERVES 4)

2 lb / 1 kg clams
3-4 slices uncooked ham
2 cloves garlic
1 large tomato
Parsley
Butter
½ cup / 120 ml white wine
½ cup / 120 ml heavy cream (in 1:1 ratio to white wine)

PREPARATION

Rinse and clean the clams.

Cut the ham into small strips and mince the garlic. Dice the tomato and chop the parsley.

Heat the butter in a pan, add the ham and brown it. Add the minced garlic and brown everything for one minute.

Add the clams, white wine, and cream and cook covered until the clamshells have opened.

Serve them with the diced tomato and chopped parsley.

THE HUNTING AND FISHING RIGHTS OF SCREEBE HOUSE COVER MORE THAN 15,000 HECTARES OF LAND AND WATER, BRINGING THE FRESHEST MEAT AND FISH TO THE INN'S TABLES.

A DELIGHT HOT OR COLD

Roast Beef in Tarragon & Red Wine Gravy

WITH MUSHROOM RISOTTO AND BLANCHED VEGETABLES

INGREDIENTS (SERVES ABOUT 10)

For the roast beef:
11 lb / 5 kg roast beef
Olive oil
Salt
Pepper

For the tarragon-red wine gravy:
2 onions
Oil
1 tablespoon dried tarragon
Juice from the roast
½ bottle red wine
Salt
Pepper
Wild mushrooms

PREPARATION

For the roast beef, brown the meat on all sides in a hot skillet with some olive oil and season it liberally with salt and pepper. Roast it slowly in a roasting pan at 165°F/75°C for 6 to 7 hours. Leave the juice in the pan.

For the tarragon-red wine gravy, peel and finely dice the onions. Sauté them in a hot skillet with some oil. Add the tarragon and the juice. Fill the skillet with red wine and reduce it by half. Season to taste with salt and pepper. Add the wild mushrooms to taste.

For the mushroom risotto:
2 onions
3½ tablespoons / 50 g butter
6 cups arborio rice
1 cup / 240 ml white wine
4¼ cups / 1 l chicken broth
½ cup / 50 g mushrooms
½ cup / 100 ml heavy cream
½ cup + 2½ teaspoons / 100 g Parmesan cheese
Salt
Pepper

For the blanched vegetables:
20 asparagus spears
1 head of broccoli

For the mushroom risotto, dice the onions and sauté them in butter in a saucepan. Add the rice to the saucepan and leave the ingredients to cook for about 1 to 2 minutes. Top this off with the white wine, stir, add the chicken broth, and keep stirring the mixture until the liquid is fully absorbed. Finally, add the cut-up mushrooms and stir in the cream and Parmesan cheese. Season the risotto to taste with salt, pepper, and butter.

For the blanched vegetables, clean the asparagus and broccoli and blanch them briefly. Serve them with the roast beef and mushroom risotto.

Vegetable Preserves

INGREDIENTS (SERVES 4)

7 oz / 200 g zucchini
7 oz / 200 g eggplant
1½ cups / 350 ml olive oil
Salt
Pepper
7 oz / 250 g red bell pepper
7 oz / 250 g yellow bell pepper
8 cloves garlic
2 lemons
1 sprig of rosemary
4 sprigs of thyme

PREPARATION

Cut the zucchini and eggplant into slices about ¼ in. / ½ cm thick. Add some olive oil to a pan, heat it, and sauté the slices in it on both sides. Season them with salt and pepper and set them aside on paper towel to remove excess oil.

Quarter the bell peppers, remove the seeds and ribs, and lay them on a baking sheet with the skin side showing. Roast the vegetables in an oven heated to about 350°F/180°C until the skins darken and blister. Take them out, allow them to cool, and remove the skin.

Now fill your canning jars, alternating between the vegetables and the garlic. Squeeze the lemons, stir some salt and the olive oil in with the juice, and fill the jars with the mixture so that the vegetables are completely covered. Scatter a few rosemary leaves over each jar, lay a sprig of thyme on the top, and seal tightly.

Kept refrigerated, the preserved vegetables will be good for about one week. To keep them for up to ten weeks, cook the jars in a pot of boiling water for 30 minutes as an additional step.

IRISH CHEESE SPECIALTIES

These popular and award-winning farmhouse cheeses are still made by hand according to the traditional method.

CASHEL BLUE
A bleu cheese made from pasteurized cow's milk. This cylinder-shaped cheese is still made with the family recipe. In its unripe form, it carries a slight fragrance of tarragon and white wine. As it ages it mellows and takes on a full-bodied, tangy flavor.

TIPPERARY BRIE
A soft cheese made from pasteurized cow's milk. Creamy and mellow in taste.

COOLEA EXTRA
A hard cheese made from pasteurized cow's milk in the style of Gouda. The *extra mature* variety ages for at least 18 months and has a very robust taste reminiscent of butter toffee.

CROZIER BLUE
Ireland's first sheep's-milk bleu cheese and to date the only one. It has a creamy and mild flavor.

BREWER'S GOLD
A semi-soft cheese made from organic cow's milk that goes well with Irish craft beer. It is intensely creamy in taste and retains a slight aroma of hops.

ST TOLA ASH LOG
A goat cheese made from raw or pasteurized milk and rolled in ashes, which slows the aging process.

ARDRAHAN
A semi-hard cheese made from pasteurized cow's milk with a washed rind. As it ages, Ardrahan becomes creamier and has a strong smell, but is mild and nutty in flavor.

INGREDIENTS FOR 4¼ CUPS / 1 LITER APPLE-ONION CHUTNEY

5 Granny Smith apples
4 shallots
Thumb's length of ginger
1⅔ cups / 400 ml water
1¼ cups / 300 ml white wine vinegar
2½ cups + 1½ tablespoons / 500 g sugar
Juice of 1 lemon
Pepper

PREPARATION

Peel the apples and cut them into small pieces; do likewise with the onions and ginger.
Add these ingredients to a saucepan and top off with the water and vinegar. Simmer the mixture for 30 minutes and season with pepper to taste. Once you have reduced the liquid, add the sugar and continue to simmer the chutney until it thickens. Allow everything to cool and serve the chutney with the cheese.

Tip: Crackers are perfect with this chutney.

FOUND EVERYWHERE, CONNEMARA'S SHEEP ARE BRED TO THRIVE IN THEIR SURROUNDINGS.

BEST WITH YOUR OWN APPLES

Irish Apple Pie

INGREDIENTS

For the filling:
10 apples
Water
2½ cups + 1½ tablespoons / 500 g sugar
1 teaspoon cinnamon
4 cups / 500 g blackberries

For the crust:
8 cups / 1 kg flour
2¼ cups / 500 g butter
2 teaspoons sugar
2 egg yolks
Water (optional)

For a 10-inch / 28 cm pie pan

PREPARATION

Peel the apples **for the filling**, cut them into pieces and add them to a pot. Add water to cover the apples. Add the cinnamon and sugar and simmer until the apples are firm to the bite. Add the blackberries at that point. Total cooking time is about 30 minutes. Let the filling cool.

For the crust, mix the flour, butter, and one egg yolk together, adding them bit by bit, and blend them to make dough. Add water if necessary.
Shape the dough into a ball and allow it to sit in the refrigerator for 30 minutes. Divide the dough into two halves. Roll out each half into a circle and line a greased pie pan with one piece.
Press the dough lightly onto the edges and bake the crust blind – in other words, line the dough with baking parchment and weigh it down with dried beans or rice – in a 350°F/180°C convection oven for about 15 minutes. Blind-baking prevents bubbles from forming in the dough and keeps the dough smooth and flat. Allow the crust to cool in the pan when it is finished baking. Pour the apple-berry mixture into the crust and cover it with the second half of the dough. Diamond or other shapes can be cut out of the remaining dough and arranged decoratively on the upper crust. Brush the entire upper crust with the second egg yolk and bake the pie for about 15 to 20 minutes until the crust turns golden brown. Best served warm with vanilla ice cream.

A Week of Good Cooking at Screebe House

DAY 3

A TRADITION NEAR AND DEAR

Full Irish Breakfast

INGREDIENTS (SERVES 4)

4 slices Irish white pudding
4 slices Irish black pudding
6 pork breakfast links (Irish bangers)
8 slices uncooked ham
7 oz / 200 g mushrooms
7 oz / 200 g cherry or grape tomatoes
8 eggs
Irish-style baked beans
Oil
Salt
Pepper

PREPARATION

Cook the black and white puddings, pork breakfast links, and ham in oil until they are browned and keep them warm over low heat.

Clean the mushrooms and cook them over medium heat with some salt and pepper, adding the tomatoes in the last minutes.

Fry the eggs sunny side up in a pan with oil. Heat the baked beans. Arrange the food on a plate and serve it.

LOCAL AND REGIONAL PRODUCTS ARE IMPORTANT TO THE CHEFS AT SCREEBE HOUSE.

RICH IN OMEGA-3 FATTY ACIDS

Gravlax

WITH HONEY-DILL-MUSTARD SAUCE

INGREDIENTS

5.3 oz / 150 g Gravlax
2 egg yolks
1 tablespoon English mustard
1 tablespoon honey
50 g dill, finely chopped
1 teaspoon whiskey or brandy
Salt
Pepper

PREPARATION

For the sauce, mix all ingredients and adjust them to taste (for example, by adding more honey or whiskey).

Serve the sauce with the gravlax.

TASTES LIKE THE SEA

Mussels in Cream Sauce

INGREDIENTS (SERVES 4)

4.4 lb / 2 kg mussels
3 cloves garlic
1½ tablespoons / 20 g butter
⅔ cups / 200 ml white wine
½ cup / 350 ml heavy cream
Salt
Pepper
½ bunch of parsley

PREPARATION

Wash the mussels and de-beard them if necessary. Discard any damaged or already opened mussels. Peel and chop the garlic. Melt the butter in a large pot and add the garlic to it. Also add the wine, heavy cream and mussels to the pot. Cook the mussels, covered, for 2 minutes, stir them, and then cook them for another 2 to 3 minutes. Serve the mussels with chopped parsley.

Quick chef's tip: The bitter-tasting filaments at the opening of the shell fasten the shell to rocks and to the ocean floor. De-bearding the mussels removes these.

IRELAND'S UNTAMED WESTERN REGIONS ARE A PARADISE BOTH FOR HIKING BUFFS AND FOR FANS OF LONELY SEASIDE VISTAS.

JUICY – TENDER – CRISPY

Connemara Lamb Chops

ENCRUSTED WITH ROSEMARY

INGREDIENTS (SERVES 4)

2.2 lb / 1 kg rack of lamb
4¼ cups / 250 g breadcrumbs
4 cloves garlic
1 handful of parsley, finely chopped
2 sprigs of rosemary, chopped
1 teaspoon prepared mustard
3 egg yolks
Oil or butter
Salt
Pepper

PREPARATION

Preheat the oven to 350°F/180°C.

Wash the meat and pat it dry, then salt, pepper and separate it.

Sauté the chops in hot oil or butter until all sides are a golden brown.

Mix the breadcrumbs, garlic, chopped rosemary, and a handful of parsley in a blender until the breadcrumbs have taken on a green color. Add the mustard and egg yolks to the mixture and stir them in.

Brush the meat with the mixture until it is completely coated and bake in the oven for 18 minutes, then allow it to cool for 4 minutes and serve.

Tip: Creamed potatoes with garlic make a good side dish. Cook the desired quantity of potatoes. Pour off the liquid from the steamed potatoes, add butter and cream for flavor, and season them with salt and white pepper to taste. Add a clove of garlic crushed with the side of a knife blade and mash the potatoes into a puree.

A TREAT FOR THE TASTE BUDS

Roasted Wild Snipe

WITH BLACK CURRANTS, PORT WINE REDUCTION AND FONDANT POTATOES

INGREDIENTS (SERVES 4)

For the roasted snipe:
4 wild snipe
Butter
4 sprigs of thyme
4 sprigs of rosemary
Salt
Pepper

For the sauce:
2 tablespoons port
1 cup / 240 ml red wine
½ cup / 100 ml black-currant jelly
1 teaspoon blackberry vinegar
1 handful of black currants
Butter

For the fondant potatoes:
4-6 medium-sized potatoes
2 cups / 500 ml chicken broth
Duck fat
Butter
Salt
Pepper
Balsamic reduction

PREPARATION

For the roasted snipe, preheat the oven to 365°F/185°C. Quickly immerse the freshly killed wild snipe in boiling water. Carefully pluck them, remove them from the water, and clean them well. Season them with salt and pepper. Push the head of each one into the thighs and breast to give it the proper form. Melt the butter in an oven-proof pan and brown the birds. Add the sprigs of rosemary and thyme and bake them in the oven for 10 minutes.

For the sauce, heat the port and red wine in a saucepan, add the black-currant jelly and vinegar, and reduce the mixture by half over medium heat. Add the black currants and some butter for flavor.

For the fondant potatoes, cut the peeled potatoes into ¾-in. / 2 cm slices; salt and pepper them.
Heat the butter in an oven-proof skillet, add the potatoes, and sear them. Reduce the heat as soon as the butter begins to bubble. Sauté the potatoes for 3 minutes on each side. Add the chicken broth and brush the potato slices with melted duck fat (or any other oil you prefer). Put the pan in an oven preheated to 375°F/190°C for 40 minutes.

Arrange the food on a plate and decorate it with the balsamic reduction.

Tip: Mushrooms and garlic bread work well with this dish.

THERE IS HARDLY ANOTHER REGION WHERE THE EMERALD ISLE SHOWS ITS CONTRASTS AS IT DOES IN CONNEMARA. SWEEPING GREEN VALLEYS ALTERNATE WITH MOORLANDS AND A ROCKY COASTLINE STUDDED WITH MANY SMALL PENINSULAS.

STILL A CLASSIC—ON THE GO TOO

Sandwich

WITH VEGETABLES AND CURRIED MAYONNAISE

INGREDIENTS (SERVES 2)

7 oz / 200 g tenderloin of Irish beef (or filet of salmon)
2 red onions
1 clove garlic, pressed
2 small dried chili peppers
½ cup / 100 ml olive oil
5 cherry tomatoes
2 tablespoons plain yogurt
2 tablespoons mayonnaise
2 teaspoons curry powder
4 slices whole-wheat toast
1 handful of baby radish or sorrel leaves
1 tablespoon fresh Italian parsley, chopped
Sea salt
Freshly ground black pepper

PREPARATION

Wash the tenderloin, pat it dry, and slice it finely. (If you are using a salmon filet, cut it into small pieces.) Finely chop a red onion and put it in a bowl together with the garlic, chili peppers, and olive oil. Add the meat (or fish), mix it gently and marinate it for at least 2 hours. Then quickly cook it in a large pan with some oil until it is done and set it aside.

Cut the tomatoes into thin slices and the second onion into thin rings. Stir the plain yogurt, mayonnaise, and curry powder together in a bowl and season with salt and pepper to taste. Toast the whole wheat bread and spread the inside of each piece with some curry mayonnaise.

Add several pieces of tenderloin (or salmon) to each piece of toast, scatter some greens over them, lay the onion and tomatoes on top of that, and finish with some parsley. Season them with salt and pepper to taste. Add the second piece of toast to make it a sandwich and cut each sandwich on the diagonal.

A Week of Good Cooking at Screebe House

DAY 4

FISHING SEASON IN THE CONNEMARA REGION RUNS FROM THE BEGINNING OF FEBRUARY TO THE END OF SEPTEMBER. SEA TROUT, NATIVE BROOK TROUT, AND NATURALLY ALSO SALMON ARE AMONG THE MOST POPULAR FISH.

FRESH-CAUGHT

Smoked Whitefish with Lemon

INGREDIENTS (SERVES 4)

4 medium-sized whitefish (such as roach, bream or barbel, gutted and cleaned with gills removed)
2 cups / 500 g coarse sea salt (more if fish are large)
Several sprigs of thyme
Several bay leaves
2 lemons

PREPARATION

Place the prepared fish in a baking dish and rub them generously with sea salt on all sides. To ensure that the fish absorb the salt evenly, marinate them for at least 3 hours—ideally overnight.

Take the fish out of the brine, rub them dry, and allow the fish to air dry (this works best if they have already been hung on smoking hooks). Then hang them in the smoker and smoke them at a high temperature. If desired, lay several sprigs of thyme and some bay leaves on the embers and cover them with sawdust.

Finish smoking and curing the fish. Take the still-warm fish out of the smoker, arrange each fish on a bed of thyme and bay leaves, sprinkle them with lemon juice, and serve them.

GUINNESS

OYSTERS

Oysters can be eaten fresh right from their shells. They contain a great deal of zinc and boost the body's defense mechanisms, which makes them a perfect food to enjoy during the winter months. Oyster enthusiasts swear by the "R" rule, which says that oysters should be bought mainly in months that have the letter "R" in their name.

Oysters should first be thoroughly washed. To open them and reach their soft center, crack the hard, sharp-edged shell. An oyster knife, which has a short blade and a sharp point, will help you to do this. You should also wear gloves. Take the oyster in your hand with the bulging side on the bottom and the flat side on the top. Now stick the oyster knife in between the upper and lower shell and turn it very slightly so that you do not damage the shell. Finally, separate the adductor muscle in the bottom shell. This will make it relatively easy to open the shell.

Galway holds its Galway International Oyster and Seafood Festival every year. Among other things, the festival features a championship in oyster shucking. The record is 30 oysters in one minute and 31 seconds.

Oysters are traditionally eaten with lemon juice.

Tip: If you cut a notch in the lemon quarter, the juice will flow in a particularly concentrated stream from the center and you will not waste any of the liquid.

SCREEB FISHER

THE WESTERN COAST OF IRELAND BENEFITS PARTICULARLY FROM THE GULF STREAM AND OFFERS UP WARM-WATER SPECIES SUCH AS MULLET, PERCH, OR AMBERJACK FOR THE DAILY CATCH.

SILVER BEL
SILVER BELL

HEALTHFUL AND FLAVORFUL

Lentils and Beets

SERVED WITH GRAVLAX AND COLESLAW

INGREDIENTS (SERVES 4)

5.3 oz / 150 g gravlax

For the coleslaw:
¼ pointed head cabbage
2 stalks dill
1 small onion
Oil
2 tablespoons balsamic vinegar
Salt
Sugar

For the lentils and beets:
1 cup / 200 g green lentils
½ onion
1 clove garlic
1 stalk of celery
1 carrot
1 small parsnip
1 fresh beet
Oil
Salt
1 pinch of sugar
Cumin
1 dash of ketchup
"Seven Spice" pepper

PREPARATION

For the coleslaw, slice the cabbage into fine strips. Chop the dill, finely dice the onion, and add them to the cabbage. Drizzle the oil and balsamic vinegar over the cabbage; mix it and season it with salt to taste. Let it sit overnight.

Soak the **lentils** to soften them. Finely dice the onion and garlic. Peel the celery stalk, carrot, parsnip and beet and cut them into a lentil-sized dice. Heat olive oil in a saucepan and sauté the garlic to a golden brown. Add salt and a little sugar. Once the garlic is golden brown, add the onions, the softened lentils, and the remaining vegetables. Cook everything over high heat until the liquid has evaporated and the vegetables begin to "sizzle". Now scatter some cumin over the glistening lentils and add a dash of ketchup and some oil. Then pour water over everything, covering the vegetables and lentils; simmer for 10 minutes. Season the lentils again with salt, sugar, and seven spice pepper to taste; turn out the lentils onto a baking sheet and let them cool.

Arrange the lentils on a plate with the beets and add the gravlax and coleslaw.

SUPPLIES PRECIOUS VITAMINS

Pumpkin Soup

WITH CROUTONS

INGREDIENTS (SERVES 4)

1 Hokkaido pumpkin
1 red onion
Olive oil
3 cups / 750 ml vegetable broth
1 can (13.5 oz / 400 ml) of coconut milk
2 slices of white bread
1 bunch of chives, chopped
Salt
Pepper

PREPARATION

Halve the pumpkin and remove the seeds (set two tablespoons of them aside and dry them on a sheet of paper towel). Wash the halves and cut them into small cubes.

Mince the onion and sauté it in a large saucepan with olive oil until it is translucent. Add the pieces of pumpkin and fill the pan with the vegetable broth to cover the contents. Simmer the pumpkin pulp over medium heat for 15 minutes until it is soft and pulpy. Puree the mixture with an immersion blender until it is smooth. Add the coconut milk, bring the mixture to a fresh boil and season it with salt and pepper to taste.

Cut the bread into cubes and brown them in a pan with nonstick coating. Then toast the pumpkin seeds and season them with salt to taste. Serve the pumpkin soup with the bread cubes, toasted pumpkin seeds, and chopped chives.

QUICKLY MADE, QUICKLY EATEN

Irish Soda Bread

INGREDIENTS

5 cups / 500 g flour, sifted
4 tablespoons sugar
1 teaspoon baking soda
1 tablespoon baking powder
½ teaspoon salt
½ cup / 120 g butter
1 cup / 250 ml buttermilk
1 egg

PREPARATION

Preheat the oven to 375°F/190°C. Mix the flour, sugar, baking soda, baking powder, salt, and butter together in a large bowl. Add the buttermilk and egg.

Take the dough out from the bowl and knead it on a slightly floured surface, but not for too long, otherwise the bread will be hard. Shape it into a round loaf and place it on a buttered baking sheet. Cut a cross into the top with a knife. Dust the loaf with flour and bake it for about 45 minutes.

Dory in White Wine Sauce

WITH CAULIFLOWER AND SWISS CHARD

INGREDIENTS (SERVES 4)

4 medium-sized John Dory or oreo dory filets prepared for cooking
2 tablespoons / 30 g butter
3 tablespoons + 1 teaspoon / 50 ml dry white wine
⅔ cup / 150 ml fish stock
Lemon juice

For the sauce:
3 tablespoons + 1 teaspoon / 50 ml court-bouillon
6 tablespoons + 2 teaspoons / 100 ml dry white wine
3 tablespoons + 1 teaspoon / 50 ml fish stock
2 egg yolks
Lemon juice
Salt
White pepper

For the vegetables:
1 head of cauliflower
8 stalks of Swiss chard
1 onion
Olive oil

PREPARATION

Season the fish filets with salt and pepper, and put them in a buttered saucepan with high sides. Add the white wine, fish stock, and some lemon juice, bring it to a boil, and simmer the fish over low heat until it is tender. Drain the court-bouillon and reduce it a little.

For the sauce, pour the white wine and court-bouillon into a saucepan and reduce it by half. Set it aside to cool. Add the liquid with the egg yolks to a double-boiler and beat them until they foam. Season them with lemon juice, salt, and pepper to taste and mix them with the reduced court-bouillon.

For the vegetables, break the cauliflower into florets, cut the thick stems off the chard, dice them, and tear the leaves into large pieces. Finely dice the onion and sauté it in a pan with olive oil until it is transparent. Add the cauliflower and chard stems and cook them over medium heat for 15 to 20 minutes, stirring. Then add the leaves of the chard and briefly cook them. Arrange the vegetables on plates, top them with the filets, and drizzle some sauce over them.

Tip: For a twist on the classic fish and chips, serve the fish with french fries.

A DESSERT FROM THE SEA

Irish Panna Cotta

WITH CARRAGEEN MOSS ALGAE AND WILD BLACKBERRY SORBET

INGREDIENTS

For the Irish panna cotta:
1½ cups / 150 g dried carrageen moss algae
2 cups / 500 ml milk
2 cups / 500 ml heavy cream
4 teaspoons honey
1 vanilla bean
Zest of one lemon
2½ tablespoons / 30 g sugar

For the sorbet:
10 cups / 1 kg blackberries
1 cup / 250 ml corn syrup
¾ cup + 1½ tablespoons / 200 ml water
¾ cup / 100 g confectioner's sugar

PREPARATION

For the Irish panna cotta, put all of the ingredients into a pot; bring them to a boil and simmer them for 2 to 3 more minutes over low heat. Then run all ingredients through a fine-meshed sieve, pour the mixture into a terrine mold, and allow it to chill in the refrigerator for at least 6 hours.

For the sorbet, put all of the ingredients into a pot, bring them to a boil, and simmer them for 2 more minutes over low heat. Then run all ingredients through a fine-meshed sieve. Pour the mixture into the ice cream maker for one hour or place it in the freezer.

IRELAND BOASTS A RICH TRADITION IN WHISKEY–IRISH MONKS ARE SAID TO HAVE DISTILLED WHISKEY AS EARLY AS THE SIXTH CENTURY. SCREEBE HOUSE HAS A SIGNATURE IRISH WHISKEY VARIETY AS WELL.

SCREEBE ESTATE
FINEST BLENDED WHISKY
LOCATED IN CONNEMARA ON THE SHORES OF WESTERN EUROPE, FAMOUS FOR ITS HERDS OF WILD RED DEER, SCREEBE ESTATE CAN BOAST OF SOME OF THE FINEST STOCK IN EUROPE, JUST LIKE THIS WHISKY, FAMOUS FOR ITS TASTE AND PREMIUM QUALITY.
AFTER A GOOD DAYS SHOOTING, RELAX AND ENJOY A UNIQUE GLASS OF SCREEBE ESTATE WHISKY BY THE FIRE.
40%vol
70cl e
FOR THE IRISH FIDDLER WHISKEY COMPANY
CONNEMARA, IRELAND

A Week of Good Cooking at Screebe House

DAY 5

THE BEST START TO THE DAY

Irish Porridge

INGREDIENTS (SERVES 1)

2 handfuls of rolled oats
1 apple
Heavy cream (to taste)
1 tablespoon dried banana chips
1 tablespoon toasted almonds
Honey, agave nectar, or cinnamon as sweetener

PREPARATION

Heat the oats and cold water in a pot (the oats should be completely covered with water). If necessary, add more water so that the oats remain covered. Bring the oats to a boil, stirring until the water has been absorbed and the porridge has a mushy consistency.

Wash and finely dice the apple. Dice the banana chips. Toast the sliced almonds. Stir in the honey, banana chips, almonds, and cream. Decorate with the diced apple and serve the porridge warm.

Variations: Top with jam or marmalade, with other fruit, or with nuts.

MINERAL-RICH CULINARY DELIGHT

Spinach-Bacon Dumplings

WITH MUSHROOM RAGOUT

INGREDIENTS (SERVES 4)

For the spinach-bacon dumplings:
1 loaf of French bread
1 slice of bacon
1 onion
3.5 oz / 100 g spinach leaves
Oil
3 eggs
1 cup / 250 ml milk
Nutmeg
Salt
Pepper

PREPARATION

For the spinach-bacon dumplings, cut one-third of the bread into cubes and fry them in butter until they are crispy. Halve and quarter the remainder of the loaf and then slice it. Dice the bacon and fry it. Sauté the onion or allow it to sweat. Cook the spinach in some oil and a bit of the diced onion, and then add the salt, pepper and some of the nutmeg.
Put the spinach in a mixing bowl and shred it with an immersion blender. Add two of the eggs and continue to puree it. Heat the milk in a pan, then set it aside. In a second pan, heat some oil, scramble one egg, and salt it.

Add the pureed spinach, the just-fried bacon, and onions (now sweated) in with the bread cubes. Also add the heated milk and the scrambled egg and mix everything gently by hand. Add some nutmeg. Keep adding enough milk to create a succulent mixture.

For the mushroom ragout:
8.75 oz / 250 g mushrooms
1 small onion
½ cup / 100 ml heavy cream
½ bunch of parsley
Oil
Salt
Pepper

Cover the bowl with the mixture and set it aside for a half hour (do not refrigerate).

Spread out a piece of plastic wrap and shape the mixture into a roll (about 1¼ in. / 3 cm in diameter). It should not result in too thick a roll—if it does, it is better to distribute the dough over several rolls. Tie the ends. Wrap the roll in foil and add it to a pot with hot water. Bring the water to a boil and simmer the roll over low heat for about 30 minutes. Take the roll(s) out and cut the dough into slices. Add oil to a pan and sauté the sliced dumplings until they are golden brown on both sides.

For the mushroom ragout, clean and chop the mushrooms. Heat oil in a pan and add the mushrooms to the pan (but only until the bottom of the pan is covered), then add salt. Dice the onion and add it to the mushrooms. Fill the pan with water or vegetable broth to cover the mushrooms. Toward the end of the cooking time, add the cream to taste, thicken if necessary, and add chopped parsley.

Arrange the dumpling slices on a plate and serve them with the mushroom ragout.

OVER 16,000 HECTARES OF LAND BELONG TO SCREEBE HOUSE, ATTRACTING HUNTERS OF HARE, WILD GOOSE, AND DEER.

FESTIVE MEAL WITH SUCCULENT GAME

Venison Stew

INGREDIENTS (SERVES 4)

For the marinade:
Bay leaves
Peppercorns
Orange zest
Lemon zest
Olive oil

For the venison stew:
3⅓ lb / 1.5 kg venison from the haunch, marinated as above
3 carrots
2 small parsnips
1 onion
1 fresh beet
4 juniper berries
1 tablespoon ketchup
2 thin slices of bacon
½ cup / 100 ml port
Sprigs of rosemary
2 bay leaves
½ cup / 100 ml red wine
Sugar
1 teaspoon berry jam
2 handfuls of ice, crushed or in cubes
Salt
Cayenne pepper

PREPARATION

Remove the sinews and skin from the meat. Sprinkle the olive oil over the meat, scatter the bay leaves, warm and halve the peppercorns, and scatter them over the meat as well. Grate the orange and lemon zest coarsely and distribute it over the meat. Cover the marinated meat and let it stand at room temperature until you are ready to work with it.

Cut the marinated venison into small cubes. Peel the vegetables and cut them into cubes of equal size. Brown the meat in a hot pan coated in oil (only add enough meat to cover the bottom of the pan, then continue to brown it in portions), and add salt and pepper. Halve the juniper berries and add them to the meat. Add the lemon/orange zest from the marinade and brown it. Take the meat out of the pan and set it aside. Sauté the vegetables in oil; add salt and pepper. Mix the meat and the vegetables and blend in the ketchup. Fry the diced bacon in a pot and gradually add in the meat/vegetable mixture.

After the first portion, add the port and wait until the liquid is reduced; add the sprigs of rosemary and bay leaves and top this off with red wine. Add the remaining meat and vegetables. Season the stew with a pinch of sugar and berry jam to taste and top it off with the crushed ice/ice cubes. Allow the stew to simmer covered for about 30 to 40 minutes. Finally, add a small pat of butter to the stew for added flavor.

THE GOLDEN EAGLE HAS ONCE AGAIN BECOME NATIVE TO IRELAND, BUT ONLY IN RECENT YEARS.

A MUST FOR AFTERNOON TEA

Scones

WITH WHIPPED BUTTER AND STRAWBERRY JAM

INGREDIENTS (YIELDS 12)

For the scones:
4¼ cups / 550 g flour
2 tablespoons + 2½ teaspoons / 2 packets of baking powder
1 pinch of salt
½ cup / 110 g butter, chilled
1¼ cups / 300 ml milk
2/3 cup / 100 g raisins
1 egg beaten with milk

For the whipped butter:
1 cup / 250 g butter, softened
1 tablespoons + 1 teaspoon / 20 ml lemon juice
2 tablespoons / 30 ml heavy cream
1 pinch salt

PREPARATION

Mix the flour and the baking powder. Add a pinch of salt, milk, and butter. Knead the dough by hand. Add the raisins to the dough and continue kneading until the dough is elastic. Dust the working area with flour and roll out the dough to a ¾-in. / 2 cm thickness. Cut out rounds with an inverted glass and arrange them on a baking sheet covered with baking parchment, leaving a good amount of space between them. Brush the scones with the egg-milk mixture and bake them in a preheated 350°F/180°C convection oven.

Whip the butter and add lemon juice and salt. Whip the heavy cream and fold it into the butter mix.

Serve the scones with strawberry jam.

COFFEE WITH SOMETHING EXTRA

Irish Coffee

INGREDIENTS (SERVES 1)

2 tablespoons + 2 teaspoons / 4 cl Irish whiskey
1 teaspoon cane sugar
⅔ cup / 150 ml coffee
Sweetened cream

PREPARATION

Warm a heat-resistant glass. Add the cane sugar and the whiskey and stir. Fill the glass with hot coffee.

Use a tablespoon to top the coffee with the semi-whipped cream, preventing them from blending.

For best results, serve hot.

A Week of Good Cooking at Screebe House

DAY 6

laoise
GALWAY

FRESH FISH

The fish market of Galway offers fresh-caught sea robin, monkfish, turbot, and much more. The diversity of species is amazing.

Scaling and Gutting

If you buy fish at the market, you should clean and eat it the same day—fish just tastes best when it is fresh. To scale it, use a dull knife, or even better, a fish scaler. Use it to scrape off the scales from the tail to the gills and from the dorsal and ventral fins without damaging the flesh of the fish. To gut the fish, make a cut along the belly of the fish starting at the anus and extending to the gills. Open the belly with your fingers and remove the entrails. Now the fish should be cleaned well under running water. Finally, remove the head with a deep cut (trout is usually prepared with the head on, so this step is skipped), and the fish is ready to be fileted.

A GAME FISH RICH IN IODINE AND ZINC

Grilled Sole

INGREDIENTS (SERVES 1)

1 filet of sole (12.3 oz / 350 g), prepared for cooking
2 tablespoons butter
Lemon juice
Salt
Pepper

PREPARATION

Wash the sole and pat it dry. Season the fish on both sides with lemon juice, salt, and pepper. Add to a baking pan with butter and grill it in a hot oven for about 5 to 6 minutes.

Tip: Serve the fish with pumpkin and cherry tomatoes.

A DELIGHT FOR EVERY SENSE

Roast Sirloin of Venison

WITH LINGONBERRY-ROSEMARY GRAVY AND POTATO PANCAKES

INGREDIENTS (SERVES 4)

For the venison:
1.3 lb / 600 g sirloin of venison
Oil for frying

For the gravy:
2 cups / 250 ml red wine
2 cups / 250 ml port
3 tablespoons red-currant jelly
1 teaspoon cornstarch
3 sprigs of rosemary
50 g fresh lingonberries

For the potato pancakes:
4 large potatoes
1 onion
1 egg
Oil
Salt
Pepper
Nutmeg

PREPARATION

Brown the venison on all sides in a pan with oil, then place it in an oven preheated to 175°F/80°C for about one hour.

For the gravy, put the port, the red wine, the red-currant jelly, and the rosemary into a saucepan and heat it until the liquid has been reduced by half; add the lingonberries, season with salt and pepper to taste, and continue to cook it for another 2 to 3 minutes.

For the potato pancakes, peel and grate the potatoes and peel and mince the onions. Mix these two ingredients, add the egg, salt, pepper, and nutmeg and stir everything together. Spoon the batter in dollops into a pan with hot oil and brown; remove the pancakes from the pan and salt them to taste.

Serve the portions of sirloin with the gravy and the potato pancakes.

indepe
connemara

Sheelin 15

5

Brewing
indepen
connemara

CONNEMARA GOLD ALE

This award-winning local beer produced by the Independent Brewing Company is a craft beer. It placed second in the Killarney Beer Awards and the Global Craft Beer Awards in Berlin. Independent Brewing produces its beers in the heart of Connemara using only natural ingredients and no chemicals or additives. With its slight touch of hops, Connemara Gold Ale tastes good with chicken, fish, and cheese. The beers of Independent Brewing are available from select online stores.

A Week
Cooking at

A Week of Good Cooking at Screebe House

DAY 7

CONNEMARA SHOWS ITS SUNNIEST SIDE IN TIME FOR THE LAST DAY.

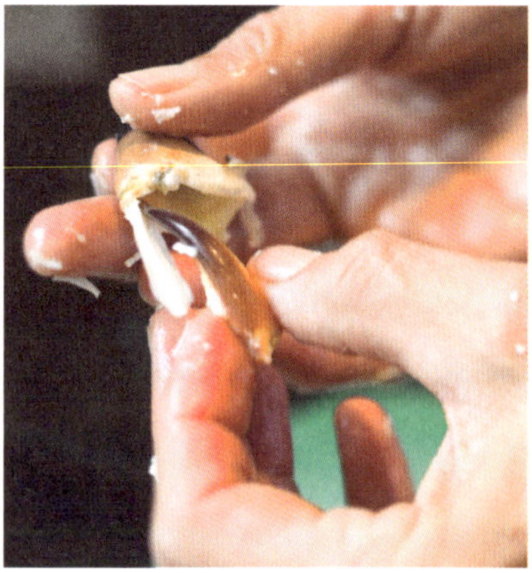

Crispy Chili-Crab Spring Rolls

INGREDIENTS

2 onions
3 bell peppers
1 carrot
1 handful of bean sprouts
1-2 small chili peppers
1 clove garlic
1 tablespoon cornstarch +
1 tablespoon water
Sweet soy sauce
Sweet chili sauce
1.3 lb / 600 g crabmeat
1 package of spring roll wrappers
Salt
Pepper
Oil

PREPARATION

Put the crabs in boiling, salted water and cook for 8 minutes. Rinse them with cold water and remove the crabmeat.

Clean and finely chop the vegetables. Dice the onions and bell peppers and quickly brown them, adding the carrots, sprouts, chili peppers, and garlic after 2 minutes. Add a dash of sweet soy and sweet chili sauces to the vegetables and season with salt and pepper to taste. Finally, stir in the crabmeat and let the mixture cool.

Unroll the spring roll wrappers. Put 1 tablespoon of filling on the lower edge of each wrapper, leaving ¾ in. / 2 cm free. Brush the edges with water. Fold the edge with the filling over first and then roll the spring roll tightly. Do the same with the remaining wrappers until all ingredients have been used up. Heat oil in a pan and fry the spring rolls in portions for 2 to 4 minutes until they are golden brown.

Venison Roulades

INGREDIENTS (SERVES 4)

For the roulades:
4 venison roulades, about 4¼ oz / 120 g per person
4¼ oz / 120 g red bell pepper
4¼ oz / 120 g zucchini
3½ oz / 100 g eggplant
2 medium-sized red onions
3 tablespoons oil
1 teaspoon ground cumin
2 tablespoons / 20 g grated Parmesan cheese
1 tablespoon tomato paste
1 tablespoon fresh marjoram, chopped
2 tablespoons hot mustard
4 slices of bacon
Flour
Salt
Pepper

For the stock:
2½ oz / 70 g carrots
2½ oz / 70 g celery root
2 teaspoons / 10 g fresh ginger
1 large onion
1 tablespoon oil
1 cup / 250 ml passionfruit juice
1 cup / 250 ml red wine
2 cups / 500 ml cherry juice
4 cloves
4 juniper berries
2 bay leaves
1 stick of cinnamon
Salt
Pepper

PREPARATION

Gently pound the **roulades** until they are flat. Clean the bell pepper, zucchini, eggplant, and red onion and finely dice them. Sauté them in 1 tablespoon of oil and season them with the salt, pepper, and cumin. Add the Parmesan cheese, tomato paste, and marjoram, and cook for another 2 minutes. Remove it from the stove.

For the stock, clean, peel, and dice the carrots, celery root, ginger, and onion. Roast the vegetables with oil in a roasting dish, season them with salt and pepper to taste, and deglaze the pan with the juices and red wine. Add the spices and simmer the stock for 5 minutes.

Brush each roulade with the mustard and lay a piece of bacon on top of each one. Spread the vegetable mixture on each one and carefully roll up the roulades, securing them with string. Roll the roulades lightly in flour and sear them on all sides in the remaining oil. Put them in the hot stock and braise them over low heat for 30 minutes. Take the roulades out of the stock and pour the stock through a sieve. Remove the string and arrange the roulades on a plate with the sauce.

Tip: Serve the dish with mashed potatoes.

FENTIMANS
FENTIMANS
EST. 1905
BOTANICALLY
BREWED
NATURAL
WILD ENGLISH
ELDERFLOWER
Fermented Botanical Drink
with Wild Elderflower Extract
275ml

SUMPTUOUS COLD DISH FULL OF VITAMIN B12

Shrimp Cocktail

WITH CHERRY TOMATOES

INGREDIENTS (SERVES 2)

1.3 lb / 600 g shrimp
2 cloves garlic
2 scallions
1 small head of romaine lettuce
6 cherry tomatoes
Several soybean sprouts
1 tablespoon heavy cream
3 tablespoons mayonnaise
1 tablespoon tomato paste
2 teaspoons lemon juice
Salt
Pepper

PREPARATION

Wash the shrimp and pat it dry. Finely chop the garlic. Cook it for about 2 to 3 minutes in a pan with non-stick coating. As it is cooking, finely chop the scallions. Remove the pan from the heat and mix the scallions together with the shrimp. Season it with salt, pepper, and lemon juice to taste. Wash the romaine lettuce and julienne the leaves. Halve the cherry tomatoes, coarsely chop the sprouts, and mix everything together in a bowl. Stir the cream, mayonnaise, and tomato paste into a dressing and season it to taste. Divide the salad between two deep glass bowls, trickle the dressing over it, and lay the shrimp on top.

RICH IN PROTEIN, IRON, AND VITAMIN B

Marinated Trout

WITH PUMPKIN

INGREDIENTS (SERVES 2)

For the trout:
2 trout filets
Dill
1 teaspoon coriander seed
1 teaspoon black peppercorns
4 juniper berries
3 tablespoons coarse sea salt
1 tablespoon brown sugar
Zest from ½ organic lemon (according to preference)
Zest from ½ organic orange (according to preference)
1 beet, raw

For the vegetables:
1 small Hokkaido pumpkin
2 small shallots
Salt
Pepper
1 teaspoon brown sugar
Cumin
Cayenne pepper (to taste)

PREPARATION

Use a pincer to remove all bones from the **trout** and gently remove any fat or skin remaining on the sides of the filet. Finely chop the dill. Warm the coriander seed, peppercorns, and juniper berries in the pan and crush them with a mortar and pestle. Add them to the herbs along with the salt, sugar, and lemon and orange zest. Mix everything well. Peel the beet and cut it into slices less than ¼ in. / 0.5 cm thick.

Lay the trout filets skin side down in a flat molded pan, lay the slices of beet on top of them, and spread the spice mixture over them in a thick layer. Depending on the thickness of the filets, leave them to marinate in the refrigerator for about one hour. Rinse the marinade off the trout with cold water, and pat it dry with a paper towel. Remove the skin and thinly slice the filets.

For the vegetables, finely dice both the shallots and the pumpkin. Brown the shallots in a pan over medium heat and add the salt, pepper, some brown sugar, and a pinch of cumin. Then put the diced pumpkin into a pan and continue to cook it until it is tender. If necessary, add salt and cayenne pepper to taste and arrange the pumpkin on a plate together with the trout filets.

FOR SPECIAL OCCASIONS

Roasted Haunch of Venison

WITH PEPPERS

INGREDIENTS (SERVES 4)

1.1 lb / 500 g haunch of venison (without bones)
1 red bell pepper
1 yellow bell pepper
Oil
Salt
Pepper

PREPARATION

Preheat the oven to 350°F/180°C.

Sear the haunch of venison in the oil on all sides. Season it with salt and pepper. Put the meat on a grille in the oven (with a baking pan under the grille to collect the liquid). After 10 minutes, turn the haunch over and leave it in the oven for another 10 minutes. Take it out of the oven, put it in an oven bag, and seal the bag. Set it aside for 30 minutes.

Clean and dice the bell peppers and sauté them in oil until they are firm to the bite. Slice the haunch of venison and serve it with the peppers.

Baked Honey-Oat Pudding

INGREDIENTS

¾ cup / 120 g dried fruit
(such as apricots, prunes, or figs)
⅓ cup / 80 ml rum
2⅓ cups / 550 ml milk
5 tablespoons sugar
4 tablespoons honey
1 teaspoon orange zest
2½ cups / 200 g oatmeal
2 tablespoons butter, plus more for the casserole dish
3 eggs
Salt

For one casserole dish with approximately 1¼ quarts / 1.2 liters of capacity

PREPARATION

Finely slice the dried fruit, place it in a bowl, and pour the rum over it. Put the milk in a pan, add the sugar, honey, and orange zest, and bring it to a boil while stirring. Remove the pan from the heat, stir in the oatmeal, and allow it to absorb the milk for about 10 minutes. Stir in the butter. Separate the eggs and stir the yolks and dried fruit into the oatmeal.

Beat the egg whites with a pinch of salt until they are stiff and fold them likewise into the mixture. Pour it into a greased casserole or pudding mold. Place this in a baking pan with high sides and fill this with boiling water so that about two-thirds of the dish or mold is immersed in the water. Bake it at 285°F/140°C for about 2 to 2½ hours.

Remove it from the oven and allow it to cool. Sprinkle some powdered sugar over the top according to your preference and serve.

A PRIVATE CONCERT ENDS A WONDERFUL WEEK.

IMPRESSIONS OF SCREEBE HOUSE

The historic Screebe House estate underwent a lavish renovation in 2010 without losing any of its antique furnishings or grand ambience. Ten luxurious rooms and suites, a spa, hunting and fishing excursions, and the inn's exquisite cuisine all promise perfect relaxation and recreation.

www.screebe.com

Index

Thank You

A very special thank you to
Laurent Burkart and Jonas Vogt-Kordes
for coordinating the week at Screebe House.

Photo Credits

Cover: © Oliver Pohlmann
Back cover: © George Karbus

Photos © Oliver Pohlmann
except
pp. 2, 4-5, 6, 8-9, 10, 100-101 © Nikolai P. Burkart
pp. 11, 50-51, 136-139, 158-159, 164-167 © George Karbus
pp. 42 (bottom) © iStock.com/Chris Gramly
pp. 92 © iStock.com/anamaria63

Oyster icon (p. 81): © Noun 454567,
created by Stephen Plaster from the Noun Project
Fish icon (p. 129): © Noun 357503,
created by icon 54 from the Noun Project
Hops icon (S. 141): © Noun 9255,
created by The Crew at Fusionary from the Noun Project
Cheese icon (S. 44): © Noun 210520,
created by Guilherme Simoes from the Noun Project
Shamrock icon (S. 166): © Noun 124377,
created by Jorge Ramiro Flores Martínez from the Noun Project
Shrimp icon (S. 19): © Noun 191042,
created by Ana María Lora Macias from the Noun Project

Imprint

Preface by Nikolai P. Burkart
Recipes by Dorothea Waydsch, Federica Fele,
Screebe House chef & Daniela Luginsland
Texts by Kerstin Buhk,
Daniela Luginsland & Nadine Weinhold
Translation by Janet Ann Golden

Editorial management by Nadine Weinhold
Design & Layout by Christin Steirat
Copy editing by Maria Regina Madarang
Production by Alwine Krebber
Imaging & proofing by Jens Grundei

Published by teNeues Publishing Group
teNeues Media GmbH + Co. KG
Am Selder 37, 47906 Kempen, Germany
Phone: +49 (0)2152 916 0
Fax: +49 (0)2152 916 111
e-mail: books@teneues.com

Press department: Andrea Rehn
Phone: +49 (0)2152 916 202
e-mail: arehn@teneues.com

teNeues Publishing Company
7 West 18th Street, New York, NY 10011, USA
Phone: +1 212 627 9090
Fax: +1 212 627 9511

teNeues Publishing UK Ltd.
12 Ferndene Road, London SE24 0AQ, UK
Phone: +44 (0)20 3542 8997

teNeues France S.A.R.L.
39, rue des Billets, 18250 Henrichemont, France
Phone: +33 (0)2 48 26 93 48
Fax: +33 (0)1 70 72 34 82

www.teneues.com

ISBN: 978-3-8327-3424-4
Library of Congress Control Number: 2016942251
Printed in Spain by Estellaprint

Bibliographic information published by
the Deutsche Nationalbibliothek.
The Deutsche Nationalbibliothek lists this publication in
the Deutsche Nationalbibliografie; detailed bibliographic
data are available in the Internet at http://dnb.d-nb.de.

FSC www.fsc.org MIX From responsible sources FSC® C009279

Enjoy with teNeues

Liora Bels

THE MIX

ISBN 978-3-8327-3381-0

Jean Christian Jury

VEGAN CUISINE

ISBN 978-3-8327-3376-6

Ben Donath, Viola Molzen

BOWL STORIES

ISBN 978-3-8327-3379-7

Gretha Scholtz

MATCHA – THE COOKBOOK

ISBN 978-3-8327-3399-5

Lohralee Astor, Tali Shine

FEEDING THE FUTURE

ISBN 978-3-8327-3343-8

Tali Shine, Steph Adams

GOOD TO GLOW

ISBN 978-3-8327-3341-4

HRH Princess Tatiana

A TASTE OF GREECE

ISBN 978-3-8327-3337-7

ALPINE CUISINE

ISBN 978-3-8327-3401-5

LIVING OFF THE LAND

ISBN 978-3-8327-3424-4